T0011660

IN RECITAL®
with All-Time Favorites

ABOUT THE SERIES • A NOTE TO THE TEACHER

In Recital® *with All-Time Favorites* is a wonderful collection of popular arrangements of children's classroom songs, traditional favorites, and the most popular folk songs ever! This series has something for everyone! Irving Berlin, George M. Cohan, and Stephen Foster are just a few of the outstanding songwriters featured in this series. The excellent arrangers of this series, Nancy Lau, Chris Lobdell, Edwin McLean, Kevin Olson, and Robert Schultz, have created engaging arrangements of some of the best All-Time Favorites, all of which have been carefully leveled to ensure success with this repertoire. We know that to motivate, the teacher must challenge the student with attainable goals. This series makes that possible. You will find favorites that are easy to sing along with as well as recital-style arrangements. This series complements other FJH publications and will help you plan student recital repertoire. The books include CDs with complete performances designed to assist with recital preparation as well as for pure listening pleasure. Throughout this series you will find interesting background information for each piece by Dave and Becky Olsen.

Use the enclosed CD as a teaching and motivational tool. For a guide to listening to the CD, turn to page 56.

THE FJH MUSIC COMPANY INC.
Frank J. Hackinson

Production: Frank J. Hackinson
Production Coordinators: Joyce Loke and Satish Bhakta
Cover Art Concept: Helen Marlais
Cover Design: Terpstra Design, San Francisco, CA
Cover Illustration: Marcia Donley
Engraving: Tempo Music Press, Inc.
Printer: Tempo Music Press, Inc.

ISBN 1-56939-791-0

ORGANIZATION OF THE SERIES
IN RECITAL® WITH ALL-TIME FAVORITES

The series is carefully leveled into the following six categories: Early Elementary, Elementary, Late Elementary, Early Intermediate, Intermediate, and Late Intermediate. Each of the works has been selected for its artistic as well as its pedagogical merit.

Book Six — Late Intermediate, reinforces the following concepts:

- Triplet and sixteenth-note patterns are used, as well as dotted-rhythmic patterns and syncopated rhythms.

- More challenging passage work, scale passages, octaves, and arpeggios.

- Pieces with changes of key, tempo, character, and articulations.

- Students play pieces in which the melody and the accompaniment are found within the same hand.

- Simple ornamentation such as grace notes are used.

- A mixture of keys strengthen the student's command of the piano.

The Saint Louis Blues was arranged as an equal-part duet. The rest of the selections are solos.

TABLE OF CONTENTS

Take Me Out to the Ball Game

Take Me Out to the Ball Game, which celebrated its 100th birthday in 2008, has been a popular favorite throughout the years, having been recorded by over 500 performers and being used in over 1,500 movies and television shows. Still, many argue that the song did not really come into its own until Baseball Hall of Fame broadcaster Harry Caray began the tradition of singing the song during a game's "seventh inning stretch" in 1971. Today, it is generally acknowledged to be the third most-performed song in America in a typical year, behind only *The Star-Spangled Banner* and *Happy Birthday to You.*

Jeanie with the Light Brown Hair

In 1854, American composer Stephen Foster wrote a song with his wife, Jane McDowall, in mind. *Jeanie with the Light Brown Hair* describes, in romantic detail, her sweet, lovely disposition and pleasing features. The song has been heard in many films over the years, and its first line was the inspiration for the 1960s television series *I Dream of Jeannie.*

When Irish Eyes Are Smiling

A light-hearted tribute to Ireland, *When Irish Eyes Are Smiling* has been recorded over 200 times by many famous artists, including Bing Crosby. Its lyrics were written by Chauncey Olcott (who also wrote *My Wild Irish Rose*) and George Graff, Jr. and was set to music by Ernest Ball. Originally composed for Ball's 1913 production *The Isle O' Dreams,* it has been used in over twenty movies and countless episodes of prime time television.

This song was known to be a favorite of President Ronald Reagan. Following the so-called Shamrock Summit–a meeting between Reagan and Canadian Prime Minister Brian Mulroney on St. Patrick's Day in 1985–the pair sang the song together at the close of the meeting. Many Canadians were displeased and Mulroney, being the son of Irish Catholic parents, was heavily criticized in the Canadian press.

ABOUT THE PIECES AND COMPOSERS

Bill Bailey, Won't You Please Come Home?

A standard with Dixieland and traditional jazz bands, *Bill Bailey*—as it is commonly known—was written by Hughie Cannon and originally published in 1902. Most often, only the chorus of the song is performed which leaves out the important information of just who Bill Bailey was and why he left home in the first place! In addition to the instrumental versions that have been recorded, Tom Chapin—a children's performer—included the song on his 2005 album *Some Assembly Required*.

Hello! Ma Baby

Written in 1899, *Hello! Ma Baby* is a song about a man who only spoke with his girlfriend over the telephone. The telephone was a fabulous "new" way of communicating, having only been invented as recently as 1876. Arguably, the most recognizable performance of *Hello! Ma Baby* was by Michigan J. Frog in the famous 1955 Warner Bros. cartoon *One Froggy Evening*.

Down in the Valley

Also known as *Birmingham Jail*, this is a traditional American folk song whose origins are unknown. Its plaintive lyrics beg that the singer not be forgotten by their true love and one of the later verses asks that a letter be sent "in care of the Birmingham Jail." In addition to being recorded by many artists over the years, this song was also included in a series of educational recordings titled *Historical America in Song* by folk singer Burl Ives in 1950.

Take Me Out to the Ball Game

Music by Albert von Tilzer
Lyrics by Jack Norworth
arr. Kevin Olson

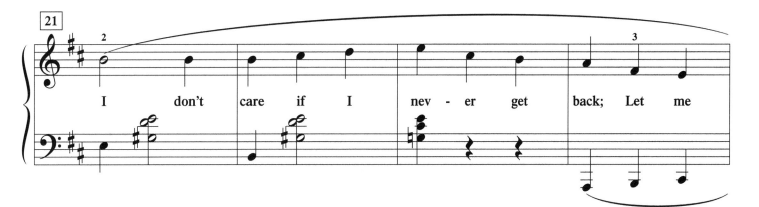

I don't care if I nev - er get back; Let me

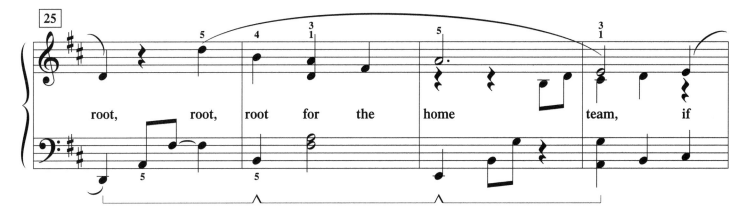

root, root, root for the home team, if

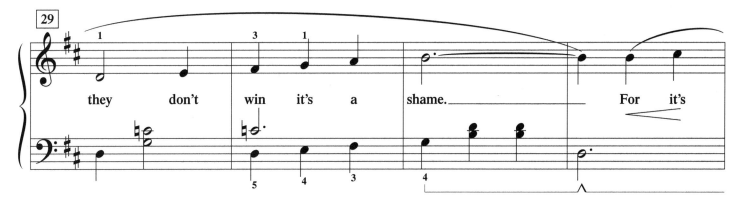

they don't win it's a shame. For it's

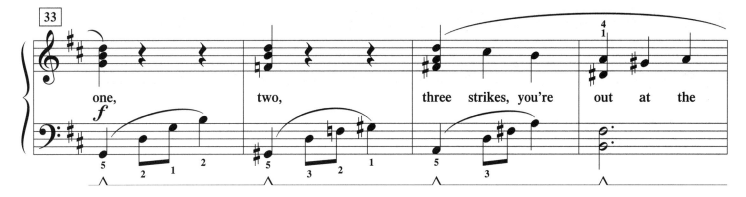

one, two, three strikes, you're out at the

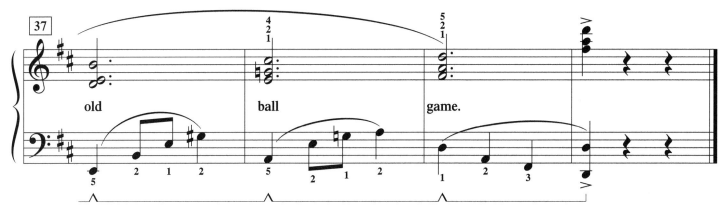

old ball game.

Jeanie with the Light Brown Hair

Music and Lyrics by Stephen C. Foster
arr. Edwin McLean

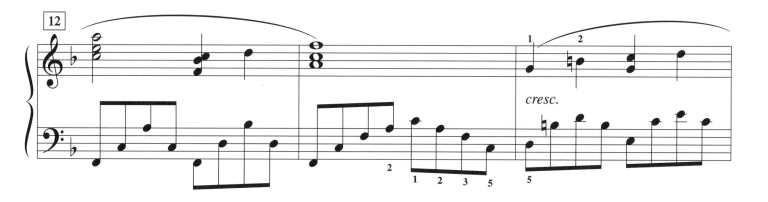

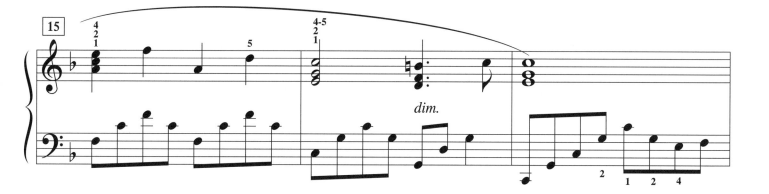

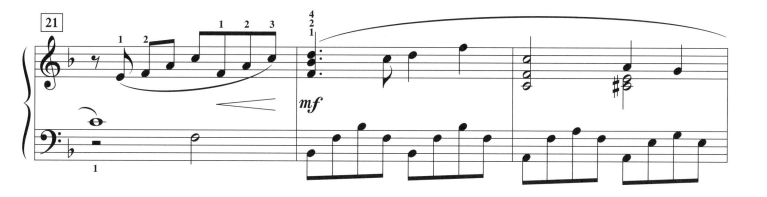

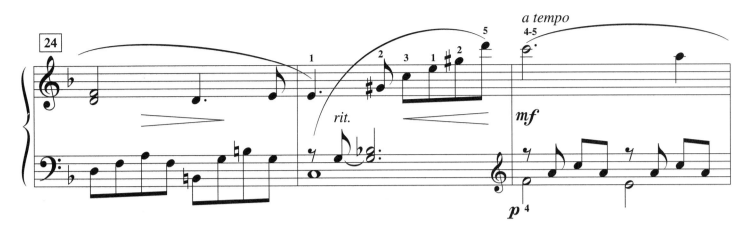

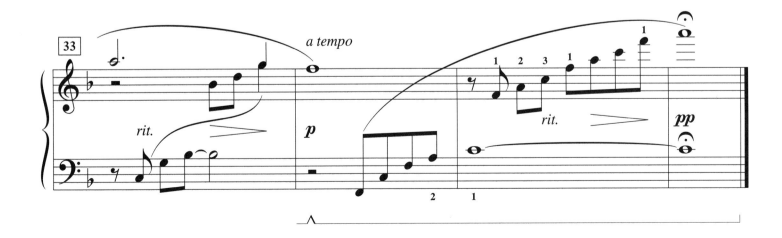

When Irish Eyes Are Smiling

Music by Ernest R. Ball
Lyrics by Chauncey Olcott and George Graff, Jr.
arr. Kevin Olson

Lightly, with a lilt (♩ = 152)

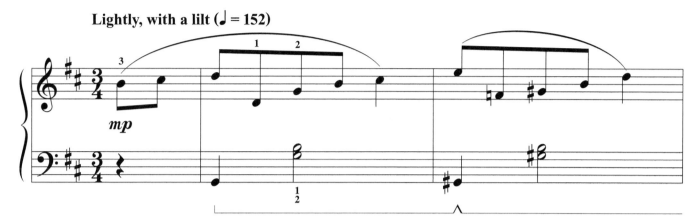

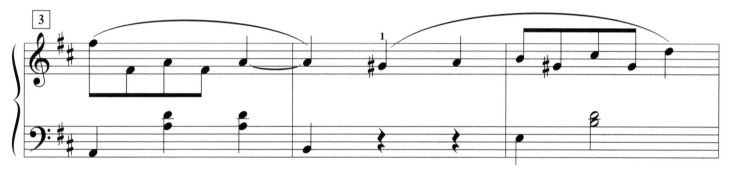

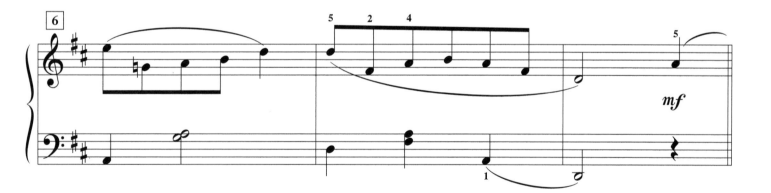

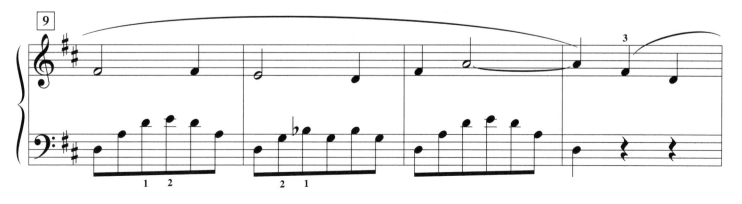

FJH2046

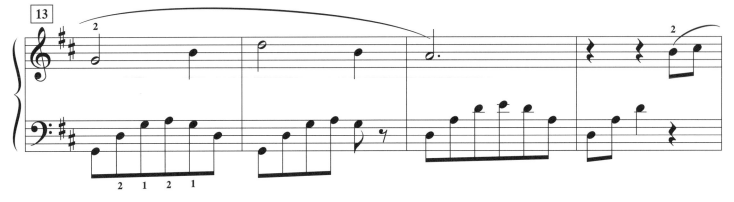

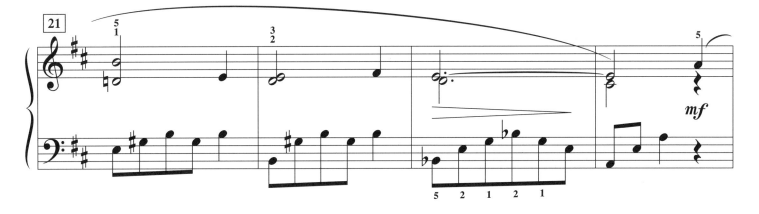

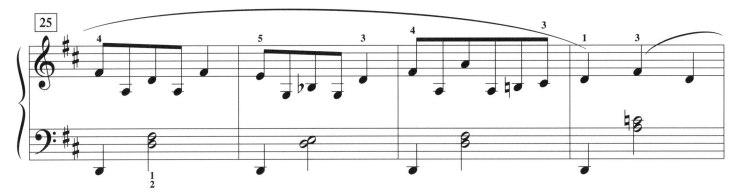

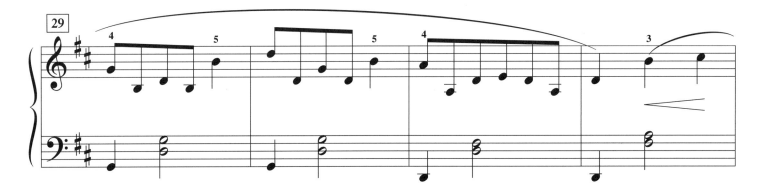

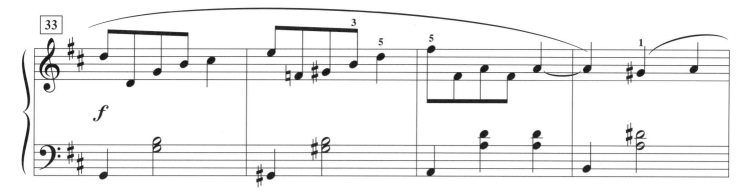

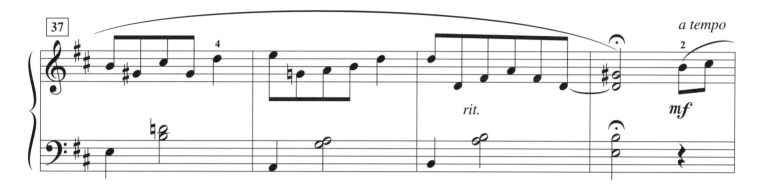

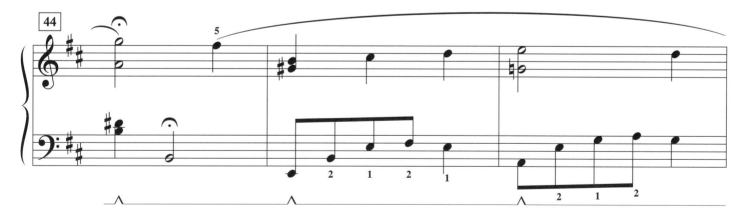

Bill Bailey, Won't You Please Come Home?

Music and Lyrics by Hughie Cannon
arr. Edwin McLean

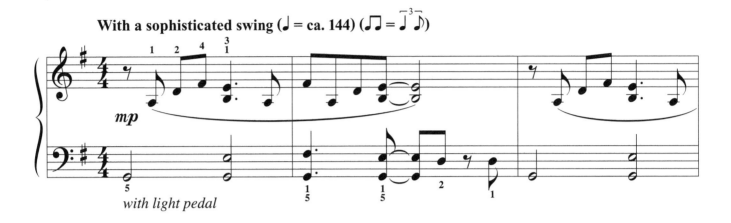

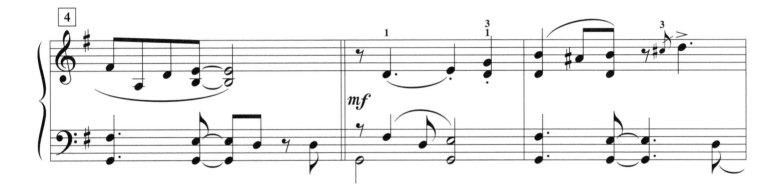

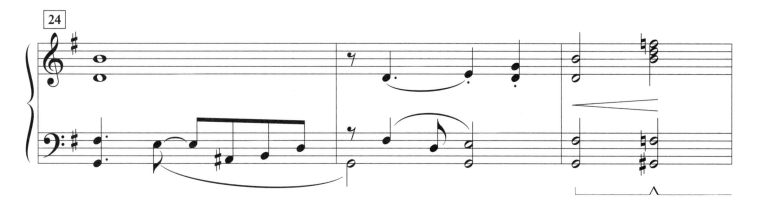

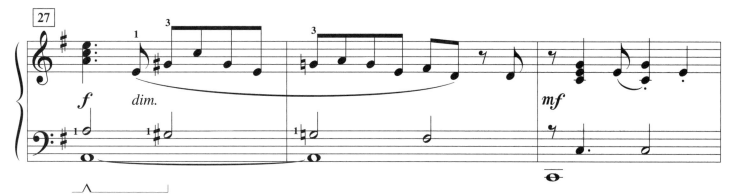

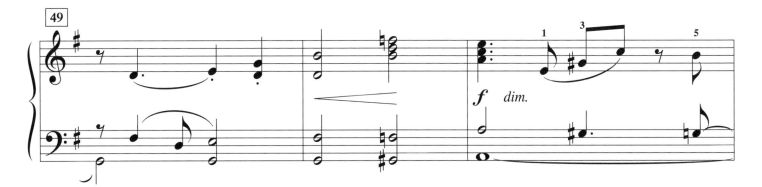

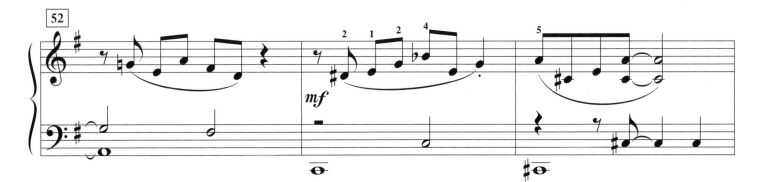

Hello! Ma Baby

Music and Lyrics by
Joseph E. Howard and Ida Emerson
arr. Robert Schultz

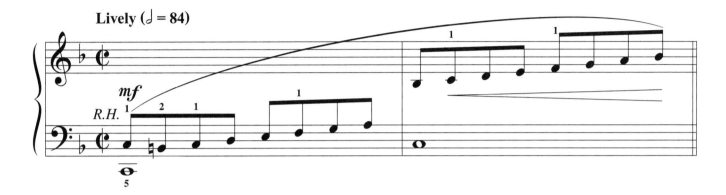

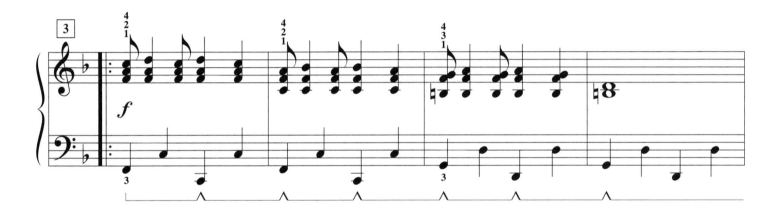

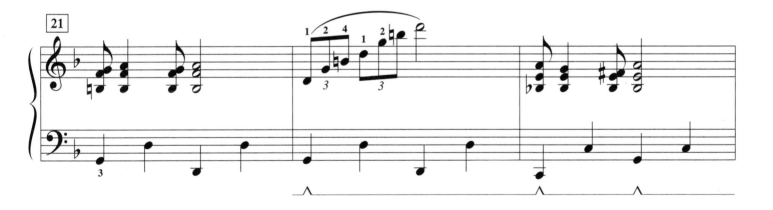

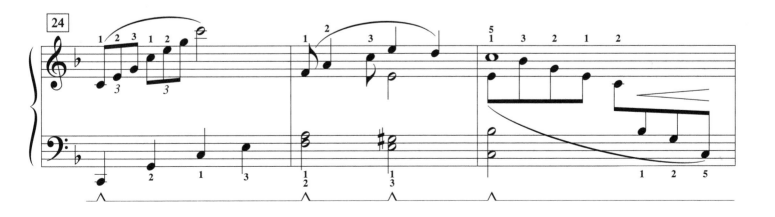

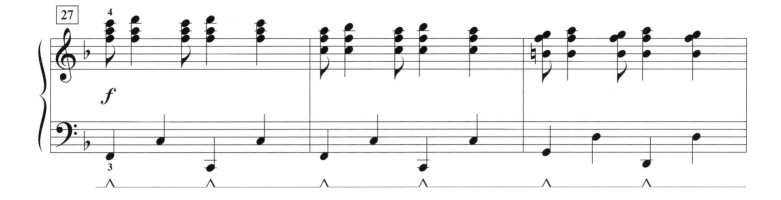

Sing-along Lyrics:

Hello! ma baby, Hello! ma honey, Hello! ma ragtime gal,
Send me a kiss by wire, baby my heart's on fire!
If you refuse me, honey, you'll lose me, then you'll be left alone;
Oh, baby, telephone and tell me I'm your own.

Down in the Valley

Traditional
arr. Edwin McLean

Country ballad, swing waltz style (♩ = ca. 126) (♫ = ♩³♪)

with light pedal

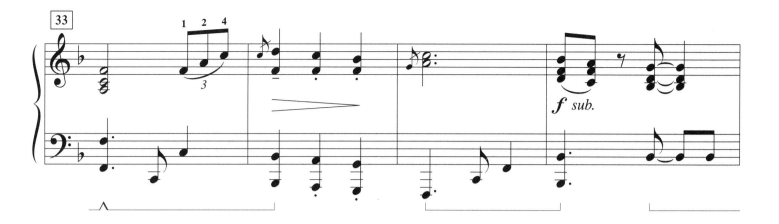

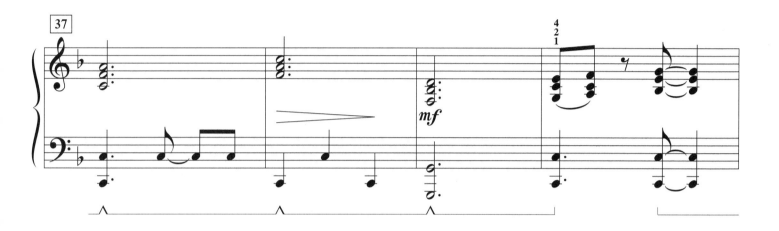

Even 8ths (no swing)

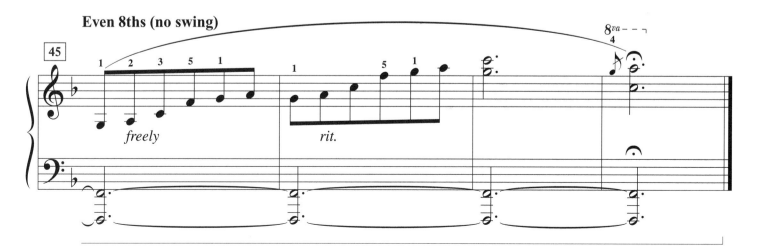

Scarborough Fair

Traditional
arr. Robert Schultz

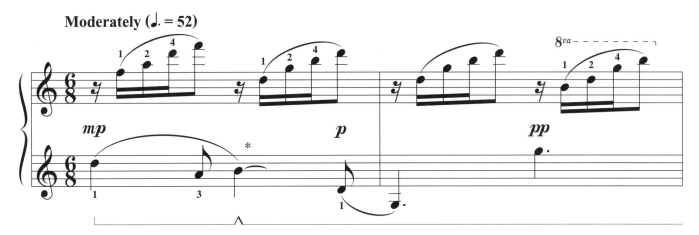

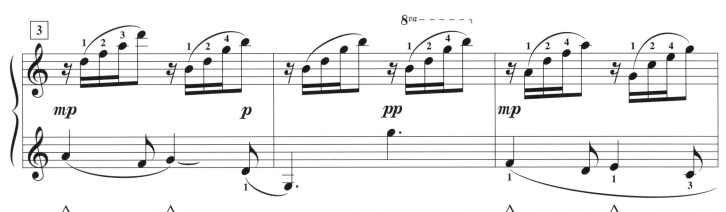

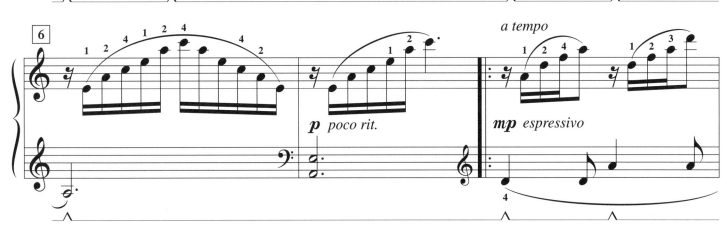

* This note should remain audible above those that follow.

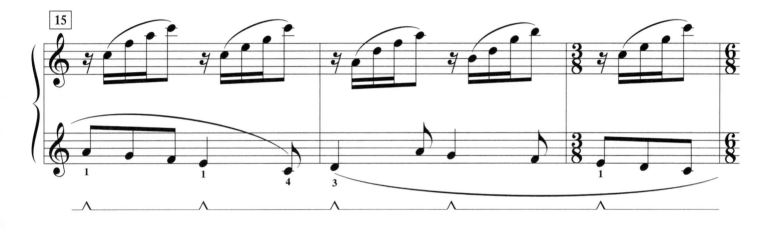

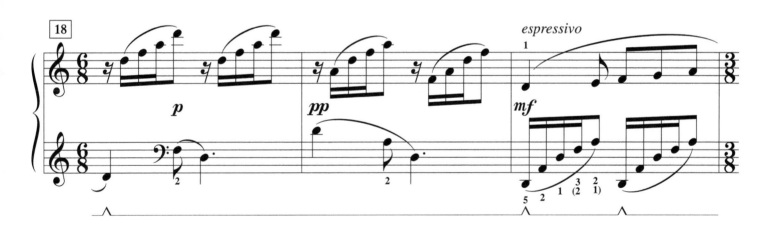

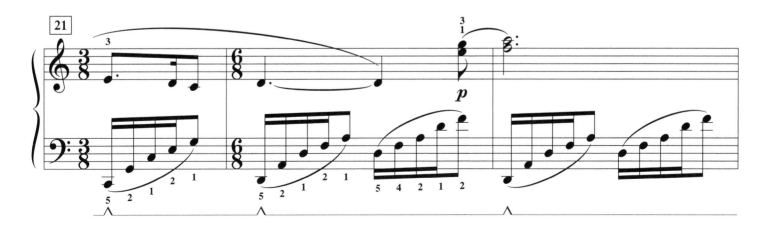

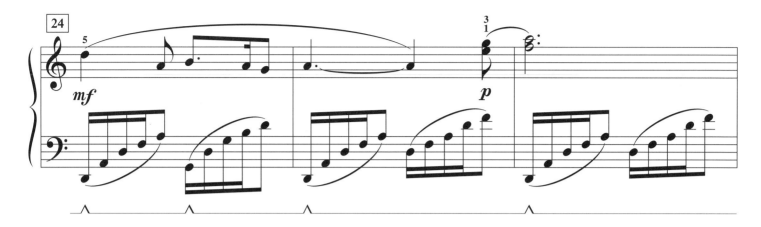

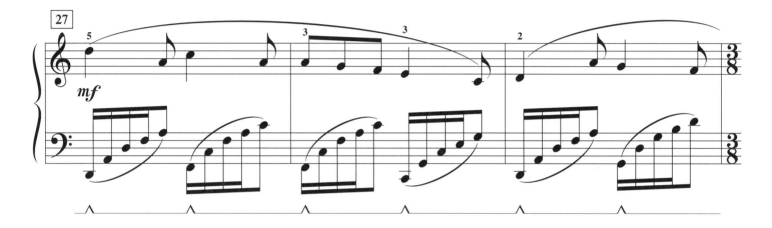

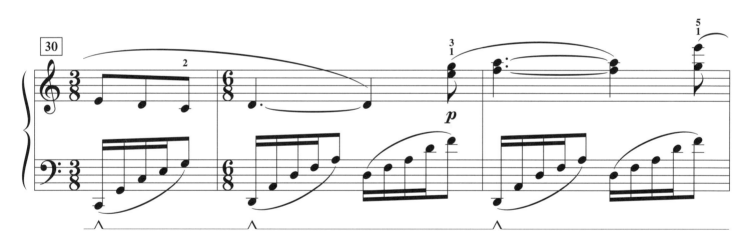

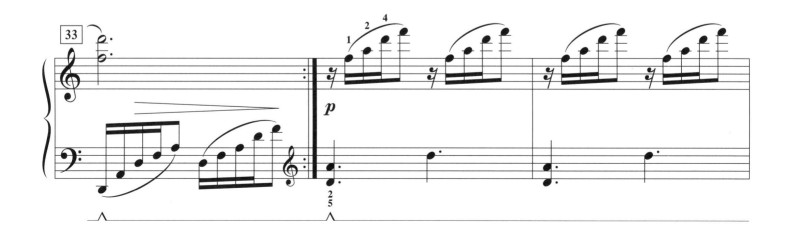

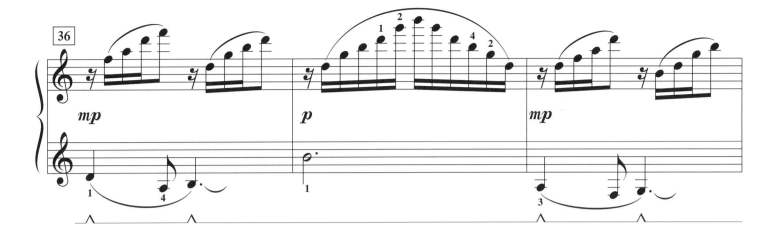

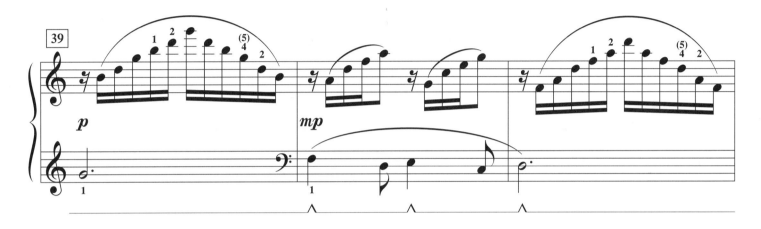

Sing-along Lyrics:

Are you going to Scarborough Fair?
Parsley, sage, rosemary, and thyme.
Remember me to one who lives there,
She once was a true love of mine.

12th Street Rag

Euday L. Bowman
arr. Nancy Lau

Allegro spiritoso ($\bf{\textstyle \bf J}$ = ca. 84)

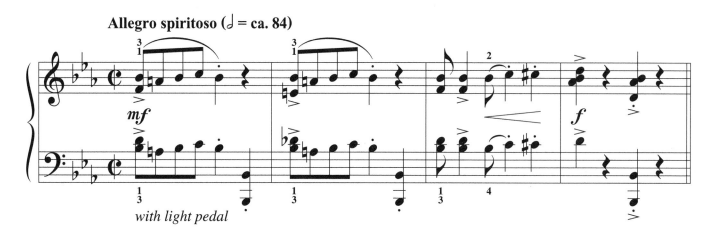

with light pedal

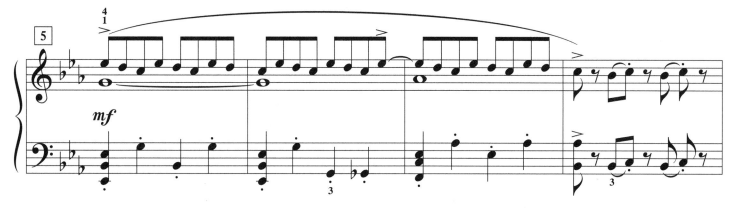

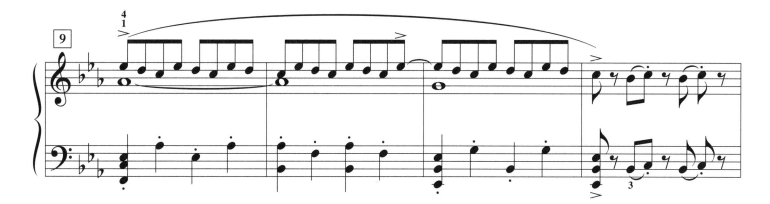

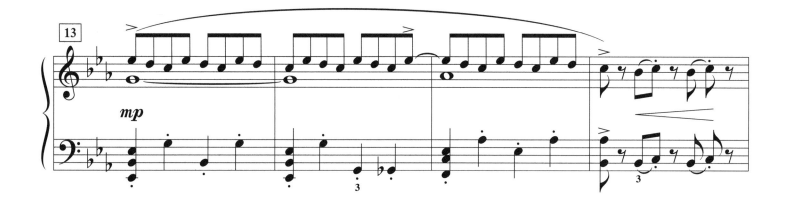

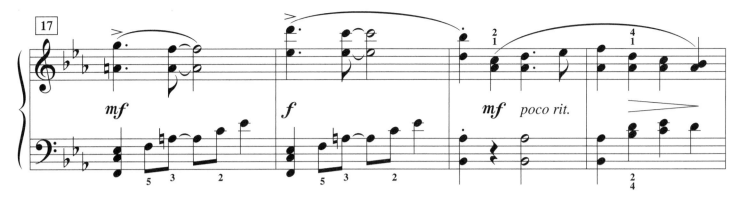

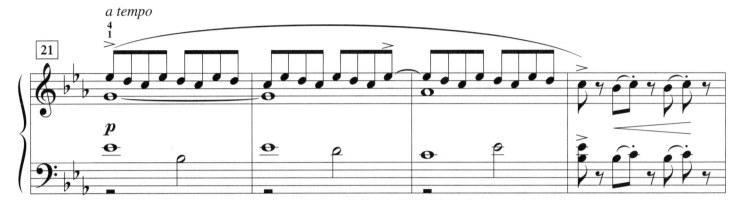

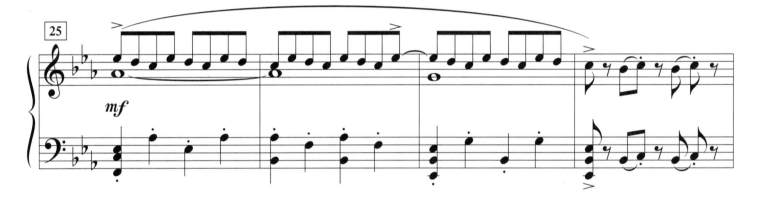

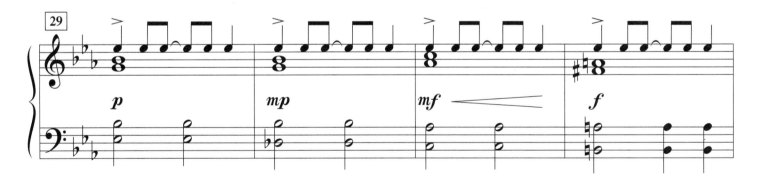

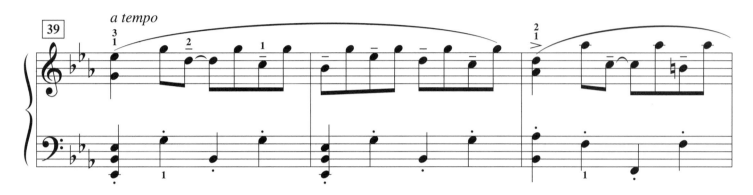

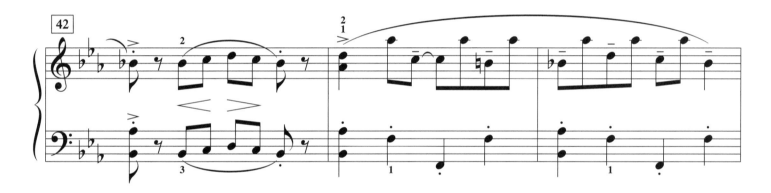

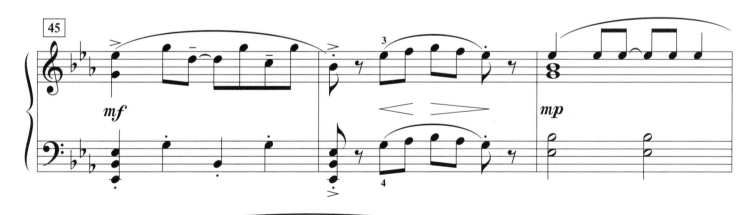

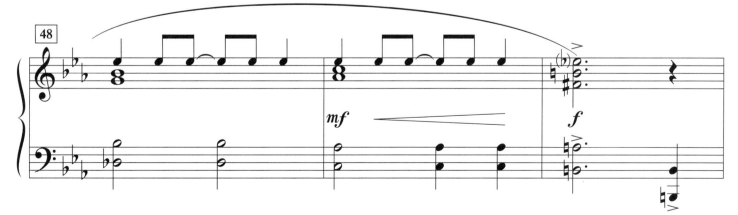

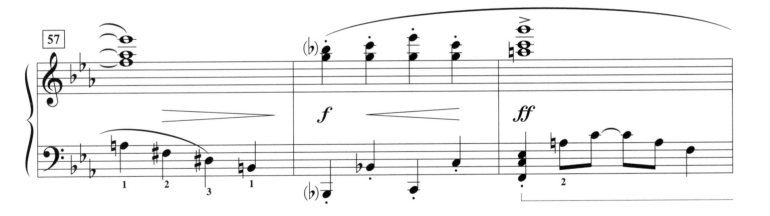

Shenandoah

Traditional
arr. Chris Lobdell

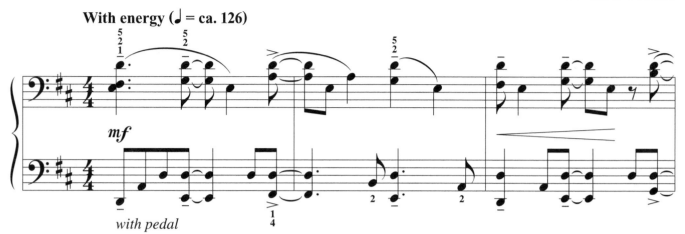

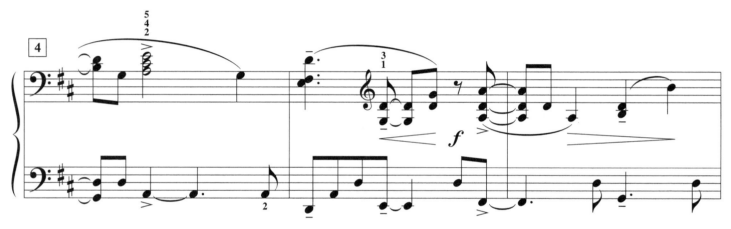

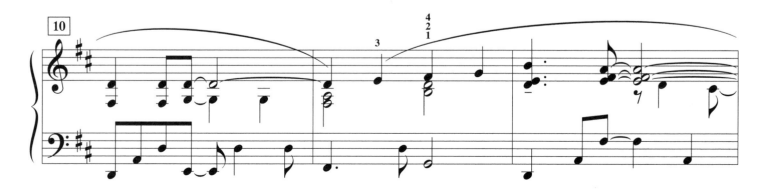

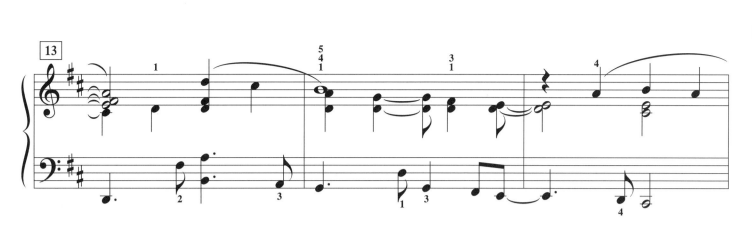

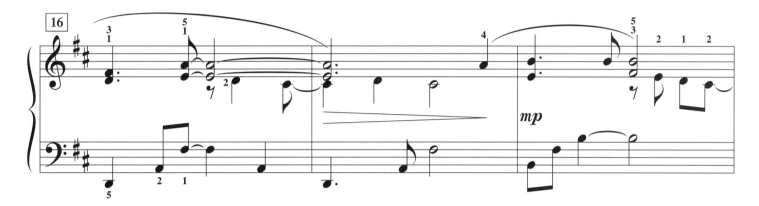

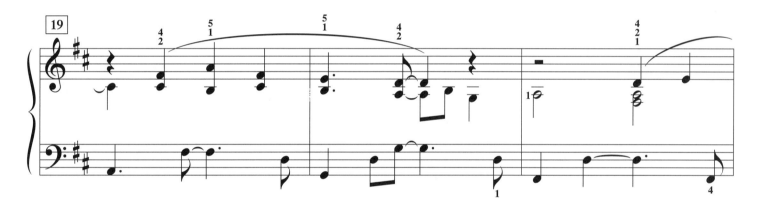

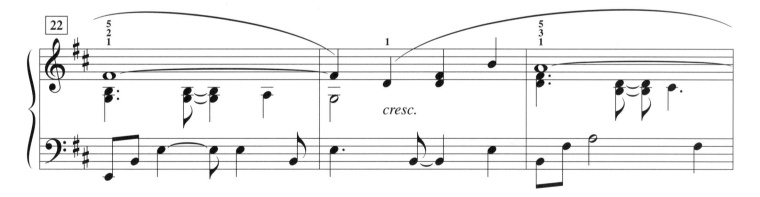

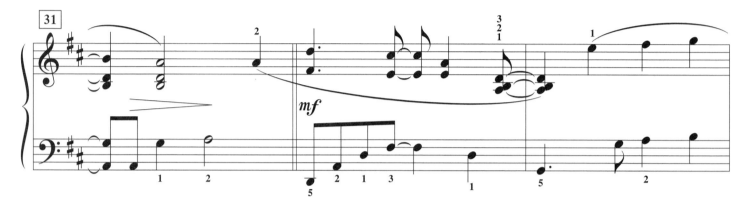

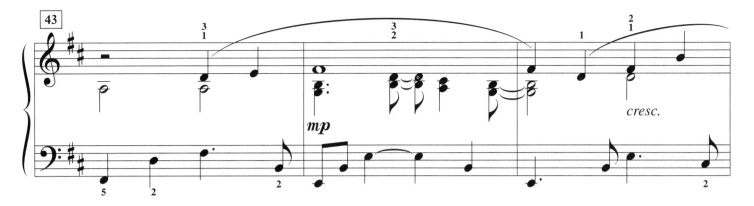

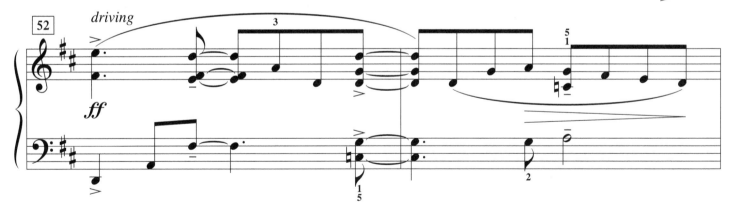

The Saint Louis Blues
Secondo

William C. Handy
arr. Robert Schultz

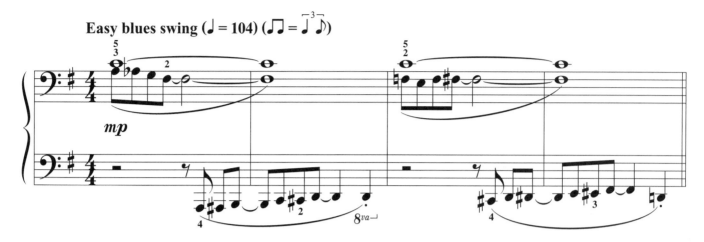

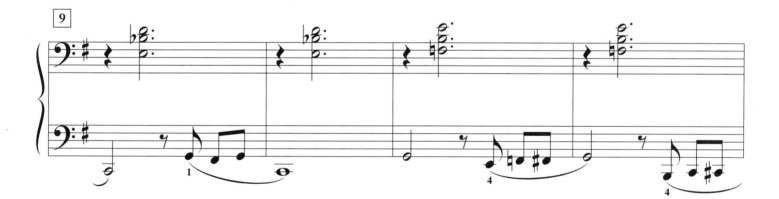

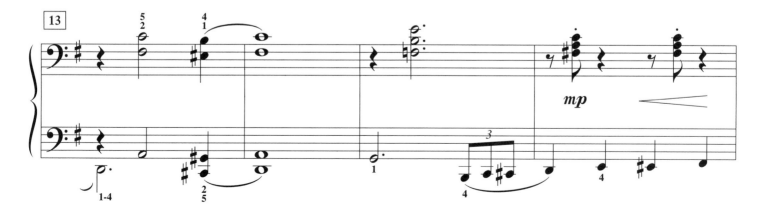

This arrangement © 2009 The FJH Music Company Inc. (ASCAP).
International Copyright Secured.   Made in U.S.A.   All Rights Reserved.

FJH2046

The Saint Louis Blues
Primo

William C. Handy
arr. Robert Schultz

Easy blues swing (♩ = 104) (♫ = ♪³♪)

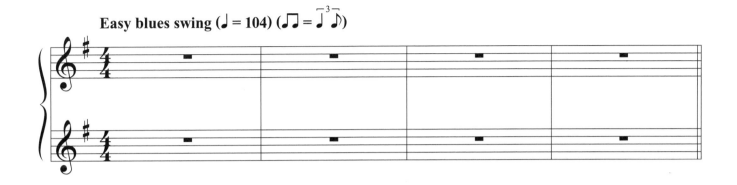

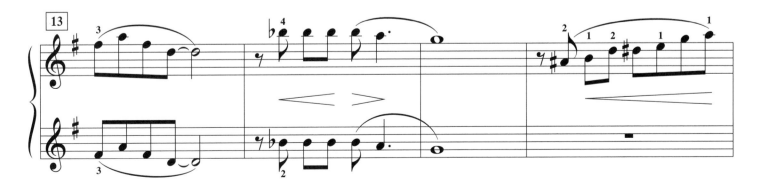

FJH2046

Secondo

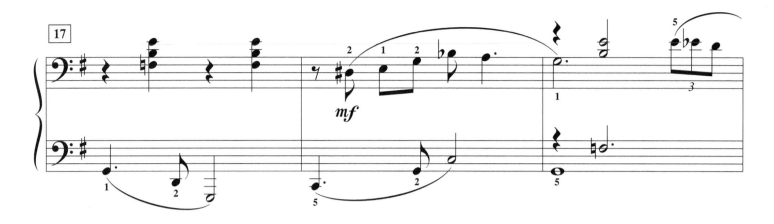

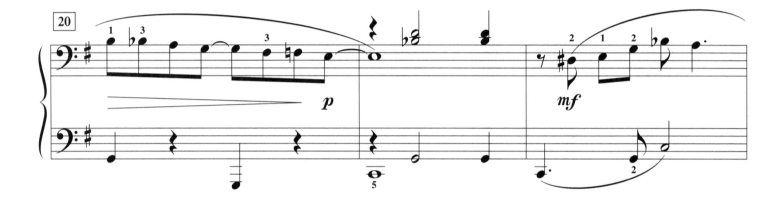

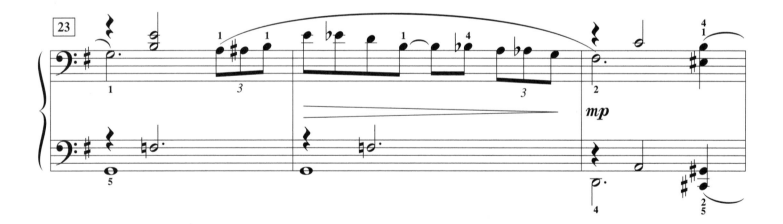

Primo

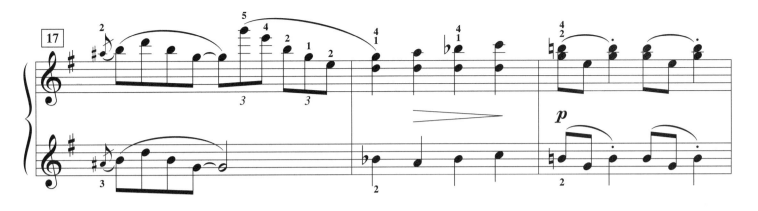

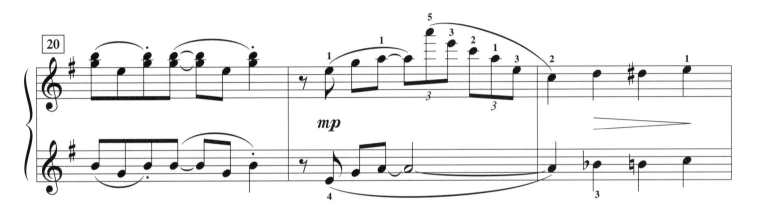

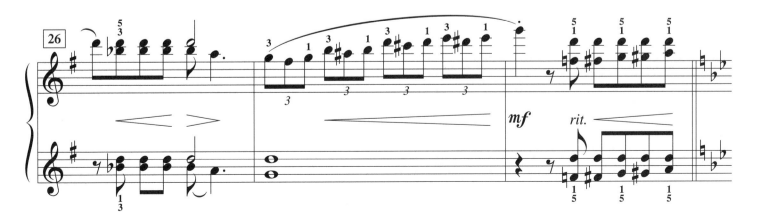

Secondo

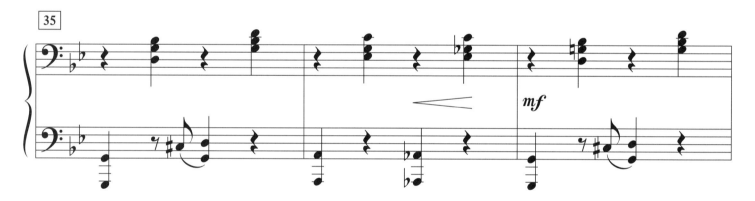

Primo

Slower (♩ = 92)

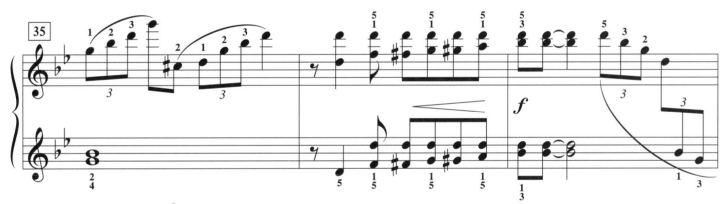

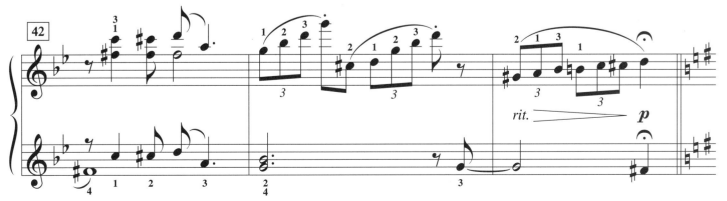

FJH2046

42

Secondo

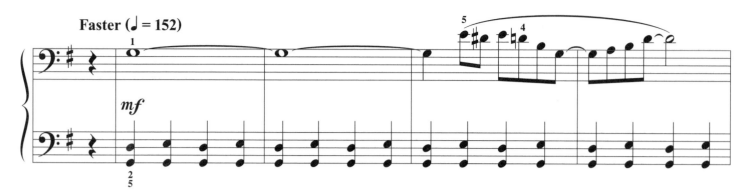

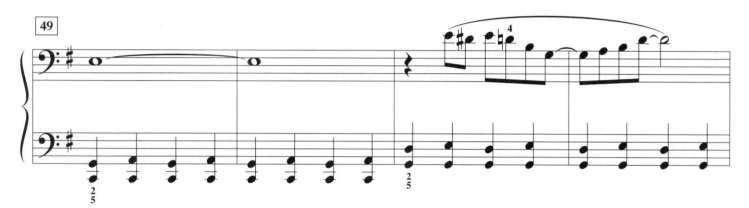

FJH2046

Primo

Faster (♩ = 152)

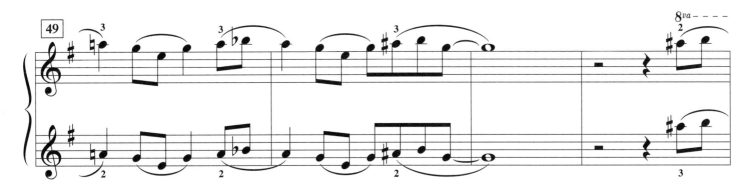

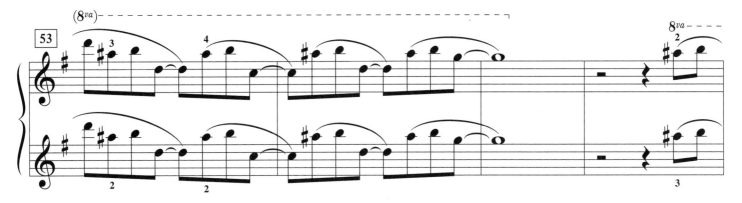

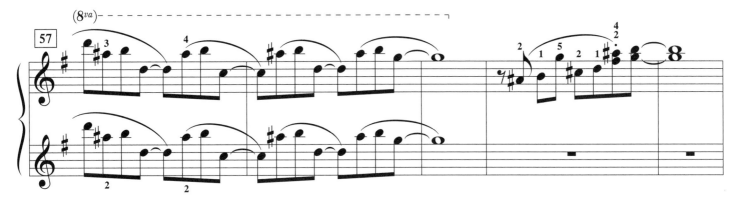

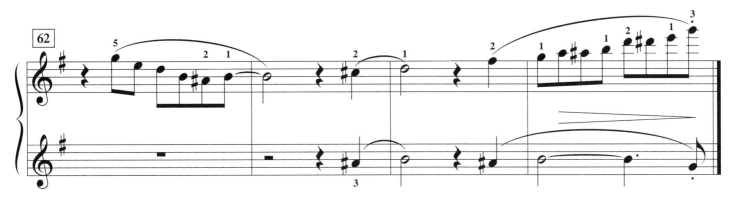

Danny Boy

Music and Lyrics
by Frederick Edward Weatherly
arr. Nancy Lau

Slowly and tenderly, with rubato (♩ = ca. 54)

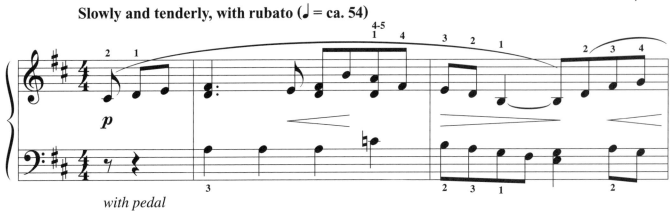

with pedal

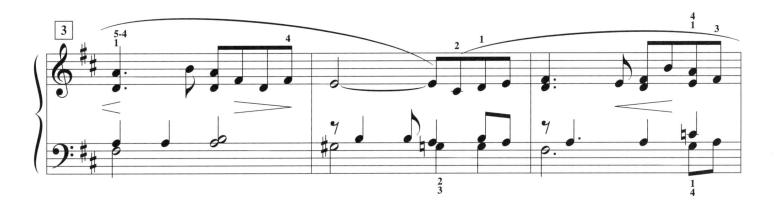

This arrangement © 2009 The FJH Music Company Inc. (ASCAP).
International Copyright Secured.   Made in U.S.A.   All Rights Reserved.

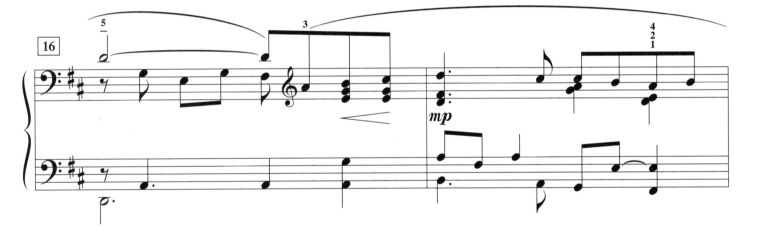

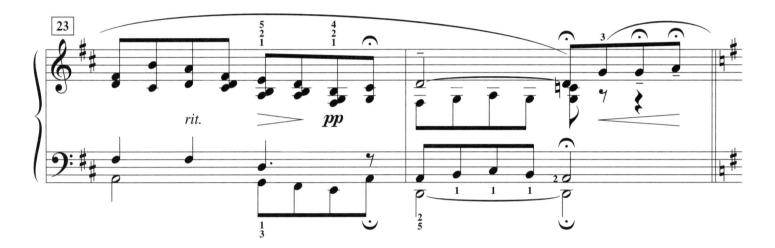

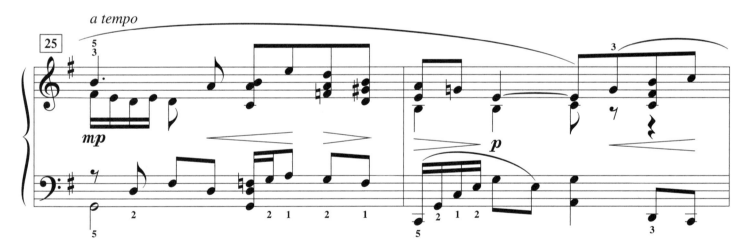

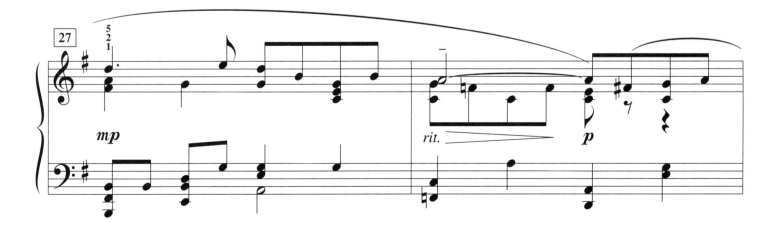

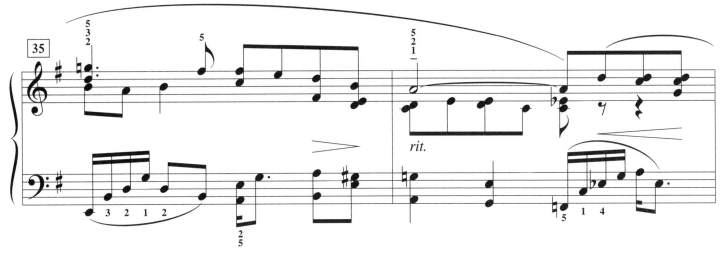

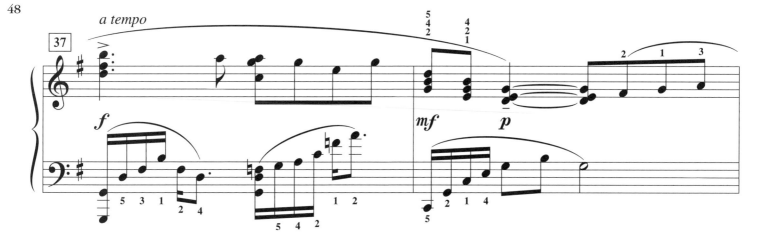

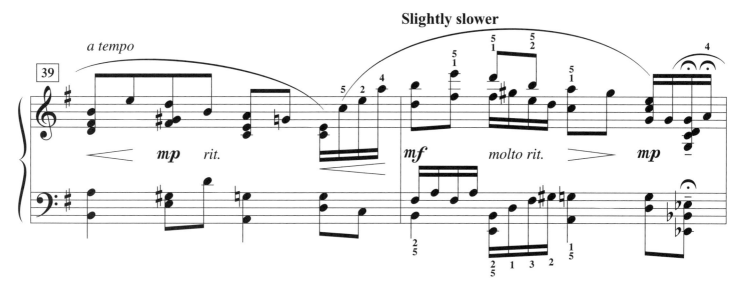

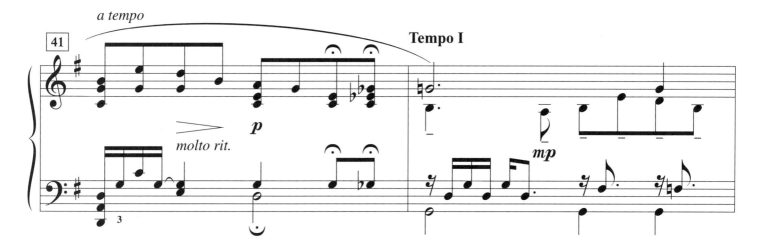

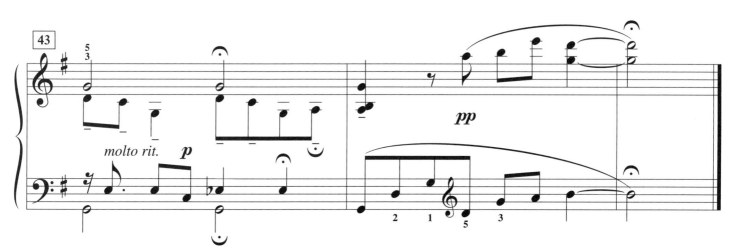

Carry Me Back to Old Virginny

Music and Lyrics by James Bland
arr. Chris Lobdell

FJH2046

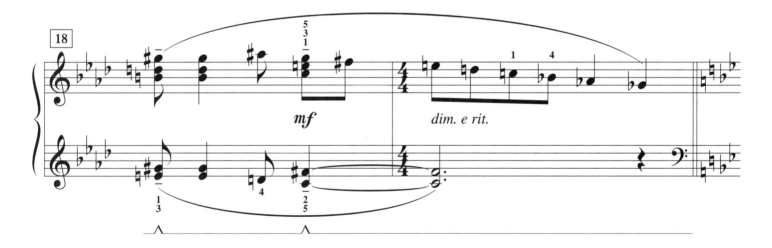

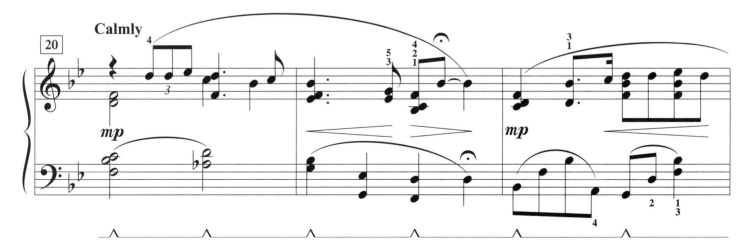

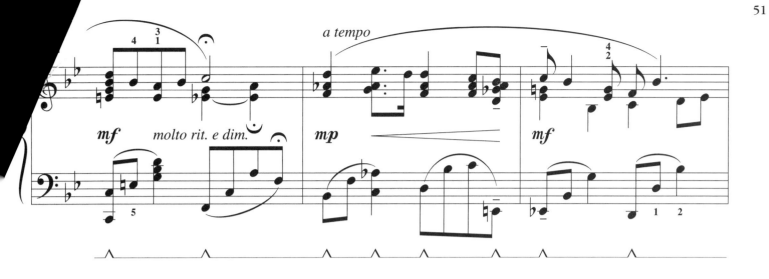

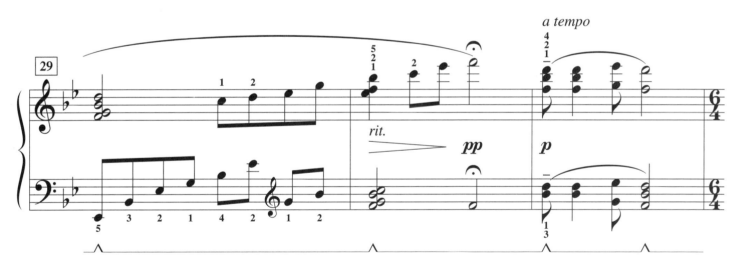

Scarborough Fair

In the Middle Ages, people did not usually take credit for songs or other works of art they produced, so the original writer of *Scarborough Fair* is unknown. This song was sung by musicians (called bards or shapers in medieval England) who went from town to town, and, as they heard the song and took it with them to another town, the lyrics and arrangements often would change. This is why there are numerous versions of this song today, and there are dozens of ways in which the words have been written down.

Even today, folk singers continue this tradition of passing songs orally to each other, though many now are able to write them down and get the credit they deserve. It was in this tradition that a British folk musician named Martin Carthy taught the song to Paul Simon, who—along with his musical partner Art Garfunkel—would further adapt the song for their 1966 smash hit record, *Parsley, Sage, Rosemary and Thyme*.

12th Street Rag

12th Street Rag was composed in 1914 by Euday L. Bowman, who was making his living traveling around the country performing as a pianist. A favorite with his audiences, he sold the copyright to *12th Street Rag* to music publisher J.W. Jenkins & Sons for the mere sum of $100. Selling copyrights was a common practice in those days. Unfortunately for Bowman, the song would go on to sell millions of copies of sheet music and piano rolls, and would become the most famous ragtime piece <u>not</u> written by Scott Joplin. A 1948 recording by pianist Pee Wee Hunt sold over three million records, and still Bowman received nothing. Years later he was able to regain the copyright, but lost out on tens of thousands of dollars in royalties.

Shenandoah

Shenandoah, sometimes titled *Oh, Shenandoah*, is a beautiful, flowing American folk song and sea chantey—a song commonly sung by sailors—which dates back to the early nineteenth century, though its origin and the true meaning of its lyrics are unclear. Some say the song tells of a roving trader who has fallen in love with an Indian princess. This may be due to the fact that the word *Shenandoah* is an American Indian word that has several meanings–including "daughter of the stars" and "deer in the woods." Others think the song tells of a pioneer of the American West longing for Virginia's Shenandoah River Valley. In 2006, the state of Virginia tried to have the song named as the state's official song, but the legislation never made it through their House of Delegates.

The Saint Louis Blues

The Saint Louis Blues is likely the most-popular and well-known "blues" song ever written. Its performers range from Louis Armstrong and Bessie Smith to the Boston Pops Orchestra. The opening line "I hate to see the evening sun go down" may well be the best-known lyric in all of popular music and set the tone for many blues tunes that followed. The song is so well established that some musicians refer to it as "the jazzman's Hamlet."

W. C. Handy said that in writing *The Saint Louis Blues* in 1914, his objective was "to combine ragtime syncopation with a real melody in the spiritual tradition." At the time of his passing in 1958, it was still earning about $25,000 annually in royalties. That's because, unlike the writer of *12th Street Rag*, Handy published the song himself and established a publishing company that to this day is operated by members of his family.

Danny Boy

Danny Boy was written by Englishman Frederick Weatherly in 1910, and in 1913 his sister changed the lyrics slightly to fit the popular tune *Londonderry Air*. Originally intended to be sung by a woman to a man, it is now most often performed by a male vocalist. Some feel the song was an homage to a son going off to war, while others think that it is more likely a memorial tribute. This song is considered an Irish anthem, but Weatherly was living in the United States at the time it was written and there is no indication that he ever visited Ireland.

Carry Me Back to Old Virginny

James A. Bland was born in 1854 in Flushing, Queens, New York and was educated at Howard University. He wrote about 700 songs during his life and performed for many years, earning the title "World's Greatest Minstrel Man." He spent twenty years performing in London alone, which included a command performance for Queen Victoria. He also toured throughout Europe, where his minstrel music was well-received. He performed in the U.S. as well, but to lesser acclaim, although many other minstrel show performers used his songs extensively. Some of Bland's songs are still heard and performed widely to this day, which accounts for his induction into the Songwriters Hall of Fame in 1970.

ABOUT THE ARRANGERS

Nancy Lau

Nancy Lau (pronounced "Law") has often been told that her music sounds very lyrical and natural. She discovered her love and talent for music early in life. Born with perfect pitch, by age four Nancy was able to play nursery rhymes on the piano by ear. She was soon coming up with her own arrangements of songs and was able to copy any music that she heard.

An active composer, arranger, and piano teacher, Nancy studied music composition with Dr. Norman Weston and piano pedagogy with Nakyong Chai at Saddleback College in Orange County, California. In addition to writing for piano, she has composed for solo voice and chamber ensemble, and has written many choral works. Her compositions have won numerous awards. Nancy maintains a full piano studio, where her emphasis is on keeping music enjoyable and exciting. She believes that students must feel nurtured and accepted, and strives to generate in her piano lessons a joyful experience and positive memory.

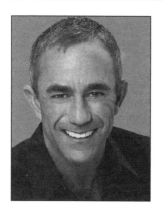

Chris Lobdell

Chris Lobdell, a native of Washington State, is nationally established as a composer-arranger, teacher, studio musician, pianist, and producer, whose compositions range from solo piano to full orchestral works. Chris has written and orchestrated for major symphony orchestras, full production shows for various cruise lines, film and video soundtracks for national television commercials, has created MIDI orchestration tracks for several piano series, and has ten years of experience as an MTNA-certified teacher. He continues an 18-year relationship with the music publishing industry as a composer, arranger, and orchestrator, and has over twenty-five books of piano arrangements in worldwide distribution.

In 1988, Chris received the U.S. President's Award for musical arrangements in the nationwide "Take Pride in America" campaign. He has served as a national adjudicator for American Guild of Music (AGM) competitions, and has been a featured presenter of technology workshops at the Florida state affiliate of MTNA and at the AGM national conference. In October of 2003, the Kirkland Orchestra commissioned Mr. Lobdell as orchestrator and featured pianist for the world premier of re-discovered works of Sergei Rachmaninoff, "Sophie's Songs."

Edwin McLean

Edwin McLean is a composer living in Chapel Hill, North Carolina. He is a graduate of the Yale School of Music, where he studied with Krzysztof Penderecki and Jacob Druckman. He also holds a master's degree in music theory and a bachelor's degree in piano performance from the University of Colorado.

Mr. McLean has been the recipient of several grants and awards: The MacDowell Colony, the John Work Award, the Woods Chandler Prize (Yale), Meet the Composer, Florida Arts Council, and many others. He has also won the Aliénor Composition Competition for his work *Sonata for Harpsichord*, published by The FJH Music Company Inc. and recorded by Elaine Funaro (*Into the Millennium*, Gasparo GSCD-331). Since 1979, Edwin McLean has arranged the music of some of today's best known recording artists. Currently, he is senior editor as well as MIDI orchestrator for The FJH Music Company Inc.

ABOUT THE ARRANGERS

Kevin Olson

Kevin Olson is an active pianist, composer, and faculty member at Elmhurst College near Chicago, Illinois, where he teaches classical and jazz piano, music theory, and electronic music. He holds a Doctor of Education degree from National-Louis University, and bachelor's and master's degrees in music composition and theory from Brigham Young University. Before teaching at Elmhurst College, he held a visiting professor position at Humboldt State University in California.

A native of Utah, Kevin began composing at the age of five. When he was twelve, his composition *An American Trainride* received the Overall First Prize at the 1983 National PTA Convention in Albuquerque, New Mexico. Since then, he has been a composer-in-residence at the National Conference on Piano Pedagogy and has written music for the American Piano Quartet, Chicago a cappella, the Rich Matteson Jazz Festival, and several piano teachers associations around the country.

Kevin maintains a large piano studio, teaching students of a variety of ages and abilities. Many of the needs of his own piano students have inspired a diverse collection of books and solos published by The FJH Music Company Inc., which he joined as a writer in 1994.

Robert Schultz

Robert Schultz, composer, arranger, and editor, has achieved international fame during his career in the music publishing industry. The Schultz Piano Library, established in 1980, has included more than 500 publications of classical works, popular arrangements, and Schultz's original compositions in editions for pianists of every level from the beginner through the concert artist. In addition to his extensive library of published piano works, Schultz's output includes original orchestral works, chamber music, works for solo instruments, and vocal music.

Schultz has presented his published editions at workshops, clinics, and convention showcases throughout the United States and Canada. He is a long-standing member of ASCAP and has served as president of the Miami Music Teachers Association. Mr. Schultz's original piano compositions and transcriptions are featured on the compact disc recordings *Visions of Dunbar* and *Tina Faigen Plays Piano Transcriptions*, released on the ACA Digital label and available worldwide. His published original works for concert artists are noted in Maurice Hinson's *Guide to the Pianist's Repertoire, Third Edition*. He currently devotes his full time to composing and arranging. In-depth information about Robert Schultz and The Schultz Piano Library is available at the website www.schultzmusic.com.

USING THE CD

A great way to prepare for your recitals is to listen to the CD.

Enjoy listening to these wonderful pieces anywhere anytime! Listen to them casually (as background music) and attentively. After you have listened to the CD you might discuss interpretation with your teacher and follow along with your score as you listen.

LISTENING ACTIVITY

Listen to the CD and circle the BEST answer:

1. **Which piece has an example of a sequence? (A sequence is when the same melodic material is repeated either higher or lower on a different note.)**

   Take Me Out to the Ball Game (Track 1)

   Bill Bailey, Won't You Please Come Home? (Track 4)

2. **Which piece has *legato* broken chords in the harmony?**

   Jeanie with the Light Brown Hair (Track 2)

   12th Street Rag (Track 8)

3. **Which piece has tempo changes?**

   Hello! Ma Baby (Track 5)

   Carry Me Back to Old Virginny (Track 12)

4. **In which piece do you hear 2-note slurs?**

   Down in the Valley (Track 6)

   Danny Boy (Track 11)

5. **In which piece do you hear syncopation?**

   When Irish Eyes Are Smiling (Track 3)

   Shenandoah (Track 9)

6. **Which piece has the form A B C?**

   Take Me Out to the Ball Game (Track 1)

   The Saint Louis Blues (Track 10)

Which piece(s) is/are your FAVORITE?

_____

_____

_____

_____

_____

_____

Answers: 1. Take Me Out to the Ball Game 2. Jeanie with the Light Brown Hair 3. Carry Me Back to Old Virginny 4. Down in the Valley 5. Shenandoah 6. The Saint Louis Blues